VISITORS ARRIVE UNCERTAIN. THEY LEAVE ENAMORED.

**Visitors arrive uncertain. They leave enamored.**
Le visiteur arrive hésitant, il repart séduit.
Los visitantes llegan perplejos. Parten enamorados.
Besucher kommen mit Zweifeln behaftet und gehen bezaubert vondannen.
Przybysze zjawiają się z wątpliwościami. Wyjezdżają zachwyceni.
I turisti arrivano incerti. Se ne vanno affascinati.
Besøkende vet ikke hva som venter dem, men reiser sin vei betatt.
半信半疑だった観光客は、魅惑されて出て行く
Οι επισκέπτες φθάνουν διστακτικοί. Φεύγουν όμως καταγοητευμένοι
방문객은 불확실함속에 도착합니다. 돌아 갈때는 매혹되어 갑니다.
疑惑的觀光者，將會陶醉的離去
疑惑的观光者，将会陶醉的离去
Konuklarimiz ne bulacaklarini bilmeden gelip, büyülenmiş olarak ayrilirlar

# Chicago, USA
# The Heart Of The Midwest.

Illinois Native American

Photographer: David J. Maenza

Written by: Jay Flynn

Designed by: James Groll

Art Direction by: Paul Collins

Edited by: Bob Hale

Associate Editor: Jeanette Rawley

Black and white photos courtesy of Special Collections Department, Chicago Public Library

WWW.CHICAGOUSABOOKS.COM

Cities are living things. Chicago's birth hides in legend and dim history. Like many cities it took its first halting steps, faltered and picked itself up again. Chicago had an unruly adolescence and then it died. Few living things rise again, especially when struck down so young. Chicago did. Not content to remain forgotten in the past, Chicago worked to fulfill a seemingly impossible future vision.

Wrigley Building and Michigan Avenue Bridge, 1900

City Neighborhood, 1865

"Back in the 1920's, my late father used to compete against Johnny Weissmuller in Chicago River marathon swims."

Norman Ross
Radio Personality

State Street, 1893

The first people to settle along the green shores of the glacier-carved lake were the Illinois native Americans. Their name for the place near the mouth of a slow river was Chicaugou. The name encompasses nothing of the city's future greatness. It means "wild onions" which grew along the marshy shoreline.

Mecca for Immigrants, 1910

Europeans first heard of Chicago from explorers and missionaries like Joliet and Marquette. Fort Dearborn was established at what is now the corner of Michigan Avenue and Wacker Drive. The first permanent European settler was Jean Baptiste Point Du Sable, a man of Franco-African descent. Du Sable came to Chicago because it stood at the head of the main trails to the unsettled west. Prophetically, he came here to trade.

Culture comes to the "Hog Butcher to the World" -- The Art Institute ca. 1920

The Reborn City grows: Turn-of-the-century parade on south Michigan Avenue

Through the early and middle 1800's the city boomed. Grain flowed out on newly built railroads. Irish, Poles, Germans, fleeing starvation and tyranny in Europe, and newly-freed African-American slaves flooded the town and Chicago sprawled into a city. Then one searing October night in 1871, the city died.

Michigan Avenue south from Chicago Avenue

Planners like Burnham and Sullivan saw an opportunity to replace disease-plagued sprawl with a model city. URBS IN HORTO, A CITY IN A GARDEN became the motto of the reborn Chicago. Its centerpiece was to be the lake shore, not acres of stone.

Chicago's Front Yard: Grant Park and "Boul Mich" District, South Michigan Avenue, 1940s

The lake shore was given over to almost 25 miles of park and recreation land, Chicago's Front Yard. Inside the city itself, 560 parks testified to the motto.

over to almost twenty-five miles of park and recreation land, which became Chicago's Front Yard. Inside the city itself, 560 parks testified to the motto.

State Street becomes "that Great Street", 1900

Sears Tower under construction, 1979

Daring architecture took root and stretched to the sky. Chicago is the birthplace of the first skyscraper and first elevated train line. Today, the works of Sullivan, Burnham and Wright stand beside those of modern architects. Mies Van Der Rohe made Chicago a proving ground of gleaming dreams in steel and glass.

Sears Tower stands as a milestone to the modern era of Chicago. Still the tallest building in the world in two official categories, Sears Tower stretches from the primeval limestone to the clouds. In its superlatives it represents leaps over countless structural obstacles that daunted those with smaller visions.

Topping this architectural giant is Sears Tower Skydeck -- "Chicago's Highest Attraction". At 1,353 feet above the ground, this world-class observatory offers stunning views covering all of Chicago and four states. High speed elevators whisk guests 103 stories skyward in just 70 seconds to where floor to ceiling windows offer unobstructed views in all directions. Since its opening on June 22, 1974, Sears Tower Skydeck has welcomed more than 30 million guests from around the world.

Sears Tower looms 1,450 feet above street level. On a clear day, parts of Illinois, Michigan, Indiana and Wisconsin can be seen from the Skydeck.

Chicago is a living museum of architecture. Walking tours criss-cross the city, showing visitors experiments and achievements of both the past and present as cranes nurse new construction skyward.

Chicagoans often play a game of guessing what a new building will look like. A castle, a geometric spire or even a wedding cake are some of the suggestions as a new iron gridwork takes shape. As the City grows, it is hard to imagine that it was nothing but ashes about 130 years ago.

"Having traveled all over the world, I know of no other city that takes as much pride in itself as Chicago. The vitality and talent of the people... and the energy, the beauty of this city, just excite me. And the climate... well, it makes you strong."

Bill Kurtis,
Award-winning broadcast journalist

Water Tower

The treasures of the past are fondly revered as new buildings are awaited. The historic Water Tower, built in 1869, best symbolizes what the city is about. It was part of the drive to modernize the booming frontier town and it survived the Great Fire, giving the people hope to rebuild. Today it stands at the head of the Magnificent Mile on Michigan Avenue.

Marking the south end of the Magnificent Mile is the Wrigley Building. Named for the chewing gum magnate, it was built in stages and finished in 1924. The limestone and terra cotta facade forms a gleaming backdrop to events on the Chicago River and the Riverwalk, where people can stroll through a ribbon of parkland all the way to the lakefront.

Wrigley Building

Like most homeowners, Chicago keeps its front yard tidy and makes it a showcase for the city.

The necessities of war have created and recreated Navy Pier. However, the city was not content to allow the mile-long building to languish into dust.

Years of reconstruction have created a family-friendly amusement and entertainment center at Navy Pier. A short ride from the heart of the city, it offers restaurants, dinner lake cruises, rides and concerts.

The revitalized Navy Pier becomes a winter playground

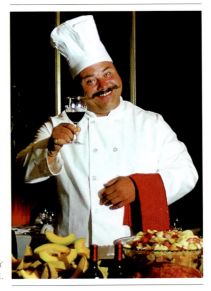

Chicago offers cuisine from every continent to suit every taste.

OLDER NEIGHBORHOODS, ONCE THE BASTIONS OF IMMIGRANTS, DOT THE CITY. FOR ITS INHABITANTS, CHICAGO IS A CITY OF NEIGHBORHOODS. EACH NEIGHBORHOOD HAS ITS OWN ETHNIC PARADES AND FESTIVALS. ST. PATRICK'S DAY FINDS THE RIVER DYED GREEN AND THE MAYOR LEADING THE PARADE THROUGH THE CENTER OF THE CITY. THE SNAP OF FIRE CRACKERS GREETS CHINESE NEW YEAR IN CHINATOWN NEAR WENTWORTH AND CERMAK. CINCO DE MAYO, POLISH CONSTITUTION DAY, OKTOBERFEST, BUD BILLIKEN DAY, FESTA ITALIANA — THE LIST IS ENDLESS.

A BUSY MAYOR LEADS ONE OF MANY ETHNIC PARADES.

The heart of the city is not just sterile steel and glass. It is a constant celebration of the soul of the city - people. Parades, festivals and music are all part of daily life in the financial and business districts of the "Loop". Even after business hours and on weekends people stay downtown for theaters, restaurants and even a ride in a horse-drawn carriage.

Fiesta on state street

Visitors also find the Chicago spirit is contagious and far-reaching. Businesses around the world are eager to share in it. Name a business or field and it probably has its convention in Chicago. Travel, sports, consumer electronics, medicine, film, autos, boats, dogs, cats, antiques are all reasons why Chicago greets more people than already live here as business visitors each year.

The crown of light at the top of the John Hancock Building can be seen from three states.

The Magnificent Mile. Chicago's premier real estate becomes a glittering ornament for the winter holidays. The display of light stretches from the river to Lake Shore Drive. A business and hotel district, North Michigan Avenue also boasts premier stores from around the world.

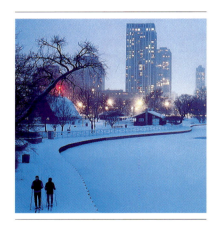

Winter can mean cold, wind and gloom. But to Chicagoans! It means hot chocolate, ice skating, tobogganing and cross-country skiing. Fun in the snow at almost any city park gives you plenty of excuses to get outdoors to try to catch snowflakes on your tongue.

The Emerald City: Chicago in winter from Lincoln Park Lagoon

"They don't call it the Windy City for nothing. But if you don't like the weather in Chicago, just wait a minute. It'll change."

Unknown

Photo of the Wrigley Building from Roosevelt Road and South Michigan avenue, 1998

All summer long, the Petrillo Band Shell in Grant Park echoes, thunders and dances to music of every taste. You can sit under the stars and let the notes flow like a cool lake breeze. Everyone comes down to the Lakefront and celebrates the Fourth of July with fireworks, food and, of course, jazz.

"When I leave this city, when I leave this earth, the one thing I'll know is this: I lived in a city that truly loved me, and I've loved them."

Michael Jordan

"I love photographing the city at night. It is like opening a chest heaped with treasure. Dazzling!"

David Maenza

State Street stores try to out-decorate each other at Christmas

South on Michigan Avenue from the Water Tower

"Hog Butcher for the World
Toolmaker, Stacker of Wheat,
Player with Railroads and the
Nation's Freight Handler;
Stormy, husky, brawling
City of the Big Shoulders;..."

Carl Sanburg
Poet

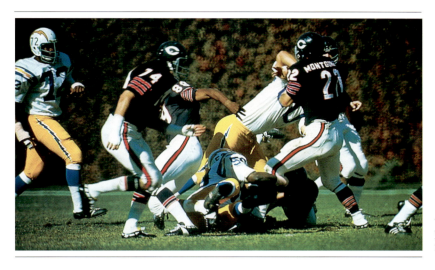

The early days of the National Football League: The Chicago Bears played at Wrigley Field.

North Michigan Avenue: Modern skyscrapers reach past the historic Water Tower like fingers to the sky.

Lakefront Joggers enjoy the sunrise in front of the newly redesigned Adler Planetarium.

"There can be no better place than this. There just can't."

Lori Garza -
Export coordinator

Gateway to the suburbs: Northwestern Train Station

"Chicago is beautiful.
Pictures don't lie."

Kimberly Gow
University student

A CIRCLE OF ELEVATED TRAIN LINES FORMS THE FAMOUS LOOP THAT CONNECTS WITH A MODERN TRANSPORTATION SYSTEM REACHING ALL PARTS OF THE CITY AND SUBURBS INCLUDING TWO MAJOR AIRPORTS.

Professional teams in every major sport excite fans in modern venues throughout the city. The Chicago Bears do battle on the grid-iron at Soldier Field. The Chicago Bulls basketball team shares the United Center with hockey's Chicago Blackhawks.

Chicago loves the national pastime so much that one baseball team is not enough.

The Chicago Cubs and White Sox play day and night games throughout the summer.

Both ballparks are located minutes away by elevated train or bus from the Loop.

Dedicated fans are not just spectators, they are part of the show at Wrigley Field and Comiskey Park.

"Alright now, let me hear ya"!
Thanks, Harry

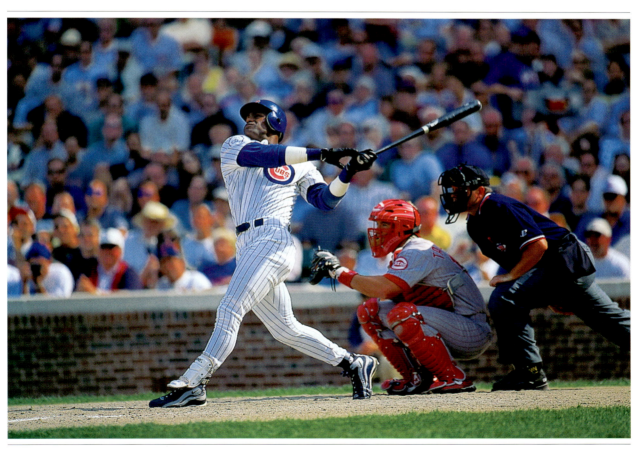

Sammy Sosa hits Number 56 on his way to a record 66 home runs. "Chicago, I love you."

"From the top of the Sears Tower, one might believe the streets are paved with gold."

Paul Collins
Designer

"Visitors arrive uncertain. They leave enamored."

Wally Philips
radio personality

The Field Museum of Natural History is a center of on-going research into dinosaurs and prehistoric man.

Chicago's heart pulses to the beat of music. Blues, Gospel, Jazz, Classical and Opera. One of the birthplaces of the fabled art, Chicago boasts Blues venues with star performers side by side with up-and-coming musicians. The Lyric Opera and Chicago Symphony Orchestra are homes to a wide range of talented artists. Music festivals for every taste span the entire year.

"Chicago writes its own music. It moves to its own beat and gets into your soul."

Bob Hale
Chicago Broadcaster

The Harold Washington Library

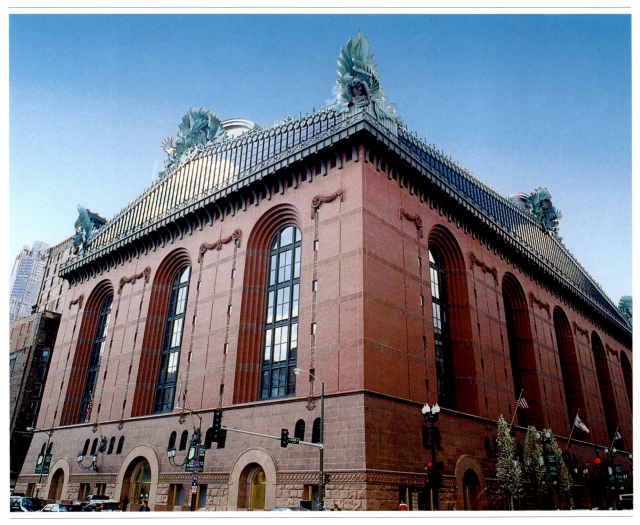

The city's mind has its needs, too. In the aftermath of the Great Chicago Fire of 1871, an Englishman, Thomas Hughes, organized the donation of 8,000 books to the city. The donations included gifts from Queen Victoria, Benjamin Disraeli, Alfred Lord Tennyson and Robert Browning. They seeded a collection that became the millions of volumes now in the Chicago Public Library's 78 locations. Acclaimed for its daring neo-classical architecture, the anchor Harold Washington Library Center at 400 S. State Street, is one of the foremost educational and cultural resources in Chicago.

"Monument with Standing Beast"
by Jean Dubuffet
at State of Illinois Building

The Chicago of stone and steel will not remain fixed forever. The seeds of the city's future are sown everyday. The skyline seems to change monthly as construction cranes pirouette to a constant, driving theme. Daring designs arc to the clouds and are filled with people with new ideas and visions.

"I love seeing Chicago change to more beautiful architecture each visit."

Daniel Beederman
Attorney

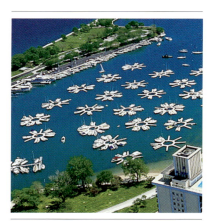

Four major marinas, serving both power and sailing craft, line Chicago's Lakefront

A lucky couple may even have Lake Michigan all to themselves.

The lake will remain. Through a miracle of engineering and the devotion of the city, the lake stays pristine, touched only by the boats who sail it and swimmers who cool off in it.

"Chicago has all the advantages of a big city and all the charm of a small town. That is the best of both worlds, and this is the best of all cities."

Joan Esposito
TV Newsperson

Marina City

Lake Michigan: Pristine waters for swimming and boating

And there will always be the parks and the design of a city in a garden. They will improve and change to fit new lifestyles and peoples.

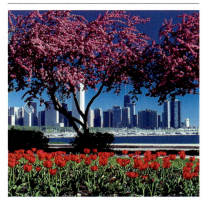

"I've been traveling the world since the early Sixties when the only thing people thought about Chicago was "Al Capone Land". Now, it's not unusual to hear first-time visitors refer to Chicago as "that wonderful city by the lake". And why shouldn't they? Ours truly is a wonderful and proud city - it is very clean with a fabulous lakefront, numerous beautifully sculpted parks and distinctive architecture.

"We have a thriving business center, world-class restaurants and, most of all, a diverse cultural community with first-rate museums, the Chicago Symphony Orchestra, the Lyric Opera, an ever-growing theater community and world-class dance companies... and I haven't even gotten to our music scene, including our much envied jazz and blues clubs.

"We are not without our problems - what major cities these days are? But the difference is that we have the courage to confront our problems and strive to work them out. We are the finest example today of great ideas and great people. We call it... Chicagoland!"

Ramsey E. Lewis Jr.

Chicago will remain dedicated to people. Those who live here and those who visit will always be able to play or work here and to find heart pounding excitement or quiet solitude.

Romantic walk: the "Golden Collar" near Lake Shore Drive.

The Heart of the City: Buckingham Fountain in Grant Park

4th of July Fireworks follow the conductor's baton to the ∼1812 Overture∼

The people are the future. They will change; new visitors and city dwellers will arrive. They will leave their mark in some way that will become inevitably Chicagoan. In exchange the "I WILL" spirit will grow into everything they do or dream.

Echoes of yesterday

"It looks like my wife."

Jack Von Buring
Construction company owner
Worms, Germany

"Beautiful? I do not know. It is like a fountain of steel."

Silvia Mendoza
Candlemaker
Mexico City

"Picasso, Miro, Chagall.... Chicago is a museum of art! The whole city!"

Penelope Mevrelos
Nurse
Athens, Greece

"The firecrackers! The food! I am so happy we were here for Chinese New Year in Chinatown. Only Shanghai would be better."

James DeGuzman
Farmer
The Philippines

Michigan Avenue Bridge over the Chicago River

"It's like a pilgrimage. We wait for that first great day in the spring and take our boats to the beautiful lake. When the last bridge goes up, we're set free."

Dr. Harold Arai
Dentist
Park Ridge

Burnham Harbor at Sunset

"Chicago is so many things. It is a harbor, a Park, big buildings .... and hot-dogs!"

Georg Garkus
Cab Driver
Russia

"It reminds me of the crown jewels in the Tower of London. It sparkles and dazzles. Diamonds, rubies and emeralds laid out at your feet."

Franklin King
Boxing Promoter
London

"It is so hard to imagine what has happened here. Nothing but marshes and grass, then came settlers with tents and shacks. And then the Fire. I wish the people standing in the ashes could see this.... who knows? Somehow maybe they did. And that is why the city's here."

Benjamin Miles
Cowboy
Minot, North Dakota

Merchandise Mart

Museum of Science and Industry

"I have to come back four more times. First time I saw just the museums. There is so much in just one of them."

Charles Farina
Boat Captain
Sardinia

"Why do they make the river green and who was this Saint Patrick?"

Dr. J. Harrani
Maldives

"The bridges are amazing! They all swing up like swans raising their necks to salute the boats."

Martha Thylin
Pharmacist
Stockholm

THE KENNEDY EXPRESSWAY HEADS IN UNDER THE CITY.

"Close your eyes and feel the city."

Lori Poppa
Accountant
Chicago

"Chicago wants you here. They want you to come. They have so many easy ways into the city. There are no walls, just the lights to guide you into its heart."

Franklin Feinberg
Investor
Tel Aviv, Israel

"Everything is so well planned and laid out. It is so convenient. All the planning of the last century has made a difference."

Erika Eddie
Property Manager
Lucerne, Switzerland

Chicago, 1980

"There is one thing about Chicago that is constant. Change. The City seems always eager to grow and outdo itself. Restless, it greets the dawn everyday with its eyes looking upward. Bigger, better, faster. It seems sometimes the energy spills over into the electrical storms that light up the sky here. In the song the city is called "toddling". Children toddle. Chicago is a large zesty youth. Its toddling days are over."

Marylin Mooney
United Kingdom

"In one word.... BOOM! Like a rocket. That's what I think of Chicago."

John Leeman
Fisherman
Nova Scotia

"I was surprised you could swim here. Not a hundred meters from a huge city and I stand in pure, clean water."

Vincent Farchie
Soccer Player
Bologna, Italy

Oak Street Beach

"At the Shedd Aquarium, they have a forest ... inside a building! It is brilliant, just how it blends right into the view of the lake."

Michael Bartley
Javelin Thrower
Cliffs of Mohr, Ireland

Shedd Aquarium

I lost my suitcase and had business at the Merchandise Mart. Fortunately, the A&G Clothing Store in the Mart had a great selection of European designs. I called Howard Goldberg at (312) 245-0377 and thanked him for all his help.

Antonio Lazzari
Rome

View into the "Loop" from the west